EDWIN NEELY

Ezekiel Explained

Getting to Know God

First published by Hayes Press 2023

Copyright © 2023 by Edwin Neely

All rights reserved. No part of this publication may be reproduced, stored or transmitted in any form or by any means, electronic, mechanical, photocopying, recording, scanning, or otherwise without written permission from the publisher. It is illegal to copy this book, post it to a website, or distribute it by any other means without permission.

Edwin Neely asserts the moral right to be identified as the author of this work.

Unless otherwise indicated, all Scripture quotations are from the New American Standard Bible® (NASB), Copyright © 1960, 1962, 1963, 1968, 1971, 1972, 1973, 1975, 1977, 1995 by The Lockman Foundation. Used by permission (www.Lockman.org).

Scriptures marked NKJV are from the HOLY BIBLE, the New King James Version® (NKJV®). Copyright © 1982 Thomas Nelson, Inc. Used by permission. All rights reserved.

Scriptures marked NIV are from the New International Version®, NIV® Copyright © 1973, 1978, 1984, 2011 by Biblica, Inc.™ Used by permission. All rights reserved worldwide.

Scriptures marked RV are from the Revised Version, 1885 (Public Domain).

Scriptures marked KJV are from the King James Version, 1611 (Public Domain).

If you enjoyed reading this book and/or others published by Hayes Press, we would really appreciate it if you could just take a couple of minutes to leave a brief review where you purchased this book.

Second edition

This book was professionally typeset on Reedsy.
Find out more at reedsy.com

Contents

1	AN INTRODUCTION	1
2	EZEKIEL'S LIFE AND TIMES	6
3	EZEKIEL'S VISIONS OF GOD	11
4	EZEKIEL'S IMAGERY AND SYMBOLISM	16
5	EZEKIEL'S VISIONS	21
6	OF HIM ALL THE PROPHETS BEAR WITNESS	26
7	GOD'S JUDGEMENT ON JUDAH AND JERUSALEM	31
8	GOD'S JUDGEMENT OF THE NATIONS	36
9	GOD'S RESTORATION OF ISRAEL	41
10	A WORD TO SHEPHERDS	46
11	THE LORD IS THERE	51
12	AN AMAZING TRANSFORMATION (KARL SMITH)	56
13	WATERS TO SWIM IN (GUY JARVIE)	59
14	A THANKLESS TASK (BOB ARMSTRONG)	63
15	EZEKIEL'S WIFE (IAN LITHGOW)	67
16	THE HANDS OF A MAN (GUY JARVIE)	70
	MORE TITLES FROM HAYES PRESS	74
	ABOUT HAYES PRESS	77

1

AN INTRODUCTION

When Judah was exiled by Nebuchadnezzar's army (circa 597 B.C.) they were settled in various places in Babylonia. Ezekiel was settled by the Chebar Canal, not far north of the city of Babylon. Their captivity differed from the latter stages of their stay in Egypt in that they were not slaves in Babylonia. They were free to integrate, build houses, run businesses, settle down and marry and be in every way part of the community, all the while obedient to its laws. Many became so much a part of things that they refused to leave when the end of the exile was announced by Cyrus some seventy years after it began.

With the northern kingdom of the ten break-away tribes being exiled to Egypt and Assyria some century earlier, and the southern kingdom, Judah and Benjamin, carried away by Nebuchadnezzar and settling in Babylonia in Ezekiel's day, and so few returning even in modern days, the large proportion of Jews have continued until now dispersed among the nations. The day will come when God will call them all back to their land, and the land will be increased in size to accommodate them.

Ezekiel was called to a life as a prophet five years after entering the land, about six before Jerusalem fell. While his bodily presence remained in Babylonia during its rule, his spirit was on occasion taken in the Holy Spirit to Jerusalem to see first-hand what was occurring (Ezekiel 8:3). The larger part of his book was uttered during his first six years of ministry. The remaining chapters, including the judgement of foreign nations and the eventual millennial restoration of Israel occur after the fall of Jerusalem. How much the foreign nations ever learned of his prophecies is questionable. He did not journey to them to present them. They certainly learned the truth of them! His ministry, even against them, was directed to the captivity in Babylonia to teach them and to instruct us.

Ezekiel, the son of Buzi, himself was from a priestly family, though the captivity meant that he never got to serve in his calling as priest. He began to prophesy at about the age of 30, when he might have been serving as priest had he been back in Israel. He is very deliberate in dating his various messages from the LORD, so we have a fairly accurate sense of the chronology of his prophetic ministry. In fact, Ezekiel has the most complete chronological outline of any Old Testament book. He ministered in Babylonia as did the prophet Daniel, (Daniel is not known in the Old Testament as a prophet, but the Lord Jesus referred to him as such in the New (Matthew 24:15)), while Jeremiah laboured among those still residing in Judah. Meanwhile, false prophets roamed both lands, even suggesting that these godly prophets were grossly misled, even mad (e.g. Jeremiah 29:24-32).

Satan saw that jealousy and hatred dogged the footsteps of the three, even of Daniel, as high up in the palace as he was, and of Jeremiah, whose prison experiences spot his jeremiad. The first part of Ezekiel's message was not nearly so well received by the people as that of the imposters. God was not saying very palatable things about his people, quite disagreeing

AN INTRODUCTION

with what the people had itching ears to hear. The life of a prophet for Ezekiel was demanding and unpopular. Jewish history reports that he was eventually slain by those that he tried to correct. His ministry lasted about twenty-two years.

The book of Ezekiel is fairly large, somewhat repetitive, and perhaps puzzling in places, but will richly reward an initial reading by those wishing to use this book as a study guide, and hopefully the chapters themselves will throw some light on what to believing Christians is a largely unread and misunderstood book. (Jewish people are taught to meditate upon it.) The key thought expressed by Ezekiel is that all who are affected by his prophecies will come to know the LORD. With slight variations, "They will know that I am the LORD," appears about seventy times. His prophetic utterances usually are introduced with, "The hand of the LORD was upon me."

This generally indicates a new vision to Ezekiel and to us. The book is really dealing with three main topics: The fall and judgement of Jerusalem; the future judgements upon neighbouring nations in all directions; and the restoration of temple, priesthood, nation and land. The chapters that deal with these topics are, more or less, 1-24; 25-32; and 33-48.

The modus operandum for this book is not a chapter-by-chapter analysis, nor a verse-by-verse exegesis. Both of those, while they might be very helpful, would be too lengthy for our present purpose. But a topic-by-topic examination of the book might fit within our parameters. The topics include this introduction; 'Ezekiel's Life and Times', to give us a flavour for the book; 'Visions of God', investigating what is revealed of deity; 'Imagery and Symbolism', looking at some of Ezekiel's methodology; 'Ezekiel's Visions', God's ways of communicating with him; 'Of Him Bare all the Prophets Witness', seeing Christ in Ezekiel; 'Judgement on Judah and Jerusalem', and lessons for our own well-being; 'Judgement on Neighbouring Nations' - how to treat those suffering God's judgements; 'The Restoration of Israel', a look at the future, glorious for Israel and for ourselves; 'A Word to Shepherds', current direction to those who assume leadership of God's people; and 'The LORD Is There', an examination of the entities that will make up the millennium in Israel; a total of eleven subjects.

Some important Messianic parts of Ezekiel are 17:22-24 where God declares that He will succeed where others such as Egypt and Babylon had failed, will plant a shoot from the very top of a cedar that will produce branches and bear fruit and become a splendid cedar; this will occur when under Messiah God's kingdom will rule the world (Daniel 2:44,45; Zechariah 14:3-9,16,17). Chapter 21:26-27 are added to that: God will "overturn, overturn, overturn" (Revised Version) "... until He comes whose right it is; and [He] shall give it to Him." This latter overturning is very much in evidence today with the insecurity and instability of the nations. Chapter 34:23-24 declares: "Then I will set over them one Shepherd, My servant David, and he will feed them; he will feed them himself and be their shepherd. And I, the LORD, will be their God, and My servant David will be prince among them; I, the LORD, have spoken."

We, too, look forward with great anticipation to that day when David's great descendant, Messiah, Christ, shall rule (Jeremiah 23:5), and one named David under Him! When all this is complete all will have a knowledge of God, from the least of men to the greatest of them (Jeremiah 31:34). Then the purposes of Ezekiel's prophecy, that men should know the LORD God will finally be complete.

In spite of people's finding the study of the book of Ezekiel somewhat daunting, there are several passages that will bring more than a flicker of recognition to the reader. These include the great mystery of the cherubim and the 'wheels within wheels' of chapter 1; the appointing of Ezekiel as a watchman to give warning from God, replete with lessons for those who should witness for Him in our day, all found in Ezekiel 3:16-21; Ezekiel chapter 11:17-20 and Ezekiel 36:26 which tell of God's New Covenant blessing of removing a stony heart from the nation and giving it a heart of flesh (Jeremiah 31:33; Hebrews 10:16); Ezekiel chapter 28:11-19 that speaks familiar words about the king of Tyre and Satan; chapter 37 which brings before us the much popularized vision of the valley of dry bones; and chapter 47 describing the ever-increasing river that will flow from the throne of God, bringing life and fruitfulness wherever it flows.

People sing about the valley of dry bones and also the stream that flows from the throne of God; they need to come to grips with what the pictures foretell and how soon it will all be fulfilled in the restoration and cleansing of Israel. We will already be in glory when that happens! The book that begins in such gloom and judgement ends in majestic glory. Praise the Lord!

2

EZEKIEL'S LIFE AND TIMES

From what at first appears to be a perplexing and frightening kaleidoscope of nightmarish and incomprehensible creatures, fearful whirling wheels and enigmatic mysteries, followed by the most ominous warnings and thundering of divine judgement, comes one of the greatest spiritual books and literary experiences of the Old Testament.

Ezekiel the priest, the son of Buzi, relates a very exact chronological history and prophecy of the post-exilic period of Israel's existence, but more importantly, clear depictions of the glory, righteousness, judgement and mercy of the God of heaven, both for his own times and for the future. Symbols and images are joined by divinely inspired parables, visions, signs, symbolic acts, direct predictions, allegories and lamentations, and out of the midst shines a radiant tapestry of the unfailing power and grandeur of divine majesty. We should not be afraid to launch out into its depths. The things that we can understand, and find benefit from, far exceed its perplexities, and even these give rich rewards in their deciphering.

Twelve of the Old Testament prophets belonged to the pre-exilic period, and five prophesied during or after the carrying away; three of the post-exilic prophets: Jeremiah, Ezekiel and Zechariah were also from the priesthood. Ezekiel was about twenty-five at the time of his confinement in 597 B.C. His actual ministry began in 593 B.C., five years after his capture. His name means 'God will harden' or 'God will strengthen', a fact borne out in his ministry; he was situated in his restraint on the banks of the drainage canal, Chebar, which flowed above the city of Babylon and connected the Tigris and Euphrates rivers. It is believed that the nobler Israelites were settled there.

His book, a highly structured and balanced work, proceeded chronologically: the first 24 chapters up until the overthrow of Jerusalem focusing on the judgement of Judah; chapters 25 to 32 on the judgement of Satan and the nations; and chapters 33 to 48 on Judah's restoration, its house, its city and its people. Judgement on Jerusalem and the peoples that were mentioned by name has been fulfilled; restoration of God's covenant people had a partial fulfilment in the remnant under Ezra and Nehemiah, and its eventual Millennial glory and conclusion await the return of a soon-coming Christ, its future fulfilment as sure as the fulfilment of the past. The departing glory of God from the house of God because of Judah's sin, visualized in chapters 9 to 11, is seen returning permanently to the house of God in chapter 43 after the infinite mercy of God has redeemed them, and Ezekiel's final victorious cry is that the glory of that city will be 'The LORD is there'.

The book is permeated with God's glory, and His actions both in judgement and in restoration are 70 times explained; He had acted so that people would "know that I am the LORD". Not only will God's elect know this, all peoples everywhere will be brought to know and acknowledge His Lordship, just as every knee in heaven and earth and hell shall one day confess that Jesus Christ is Lord, to the glory of God the Father (Philippians 2:10,11).

Ezekiel's recorded ministry was largely one of judgement because of arrogant sin, but the judgement of God is always mingled with mercy. His written work covered a period of about twenty-two years from 593 to 571 B.C. His ministry was doubtless the catalyst that caused Israel to be purged from their idolatry. That failing would be unknown in Israel following the exile. Over ninety times during the book he is referred to as 'son of man', emphasizing that he was of the order of humanity, replete with its weakness and dependence upon God. To Daniel this term was applied once (Daniel 8:17). Later the term 'the Son of Man' became a messianic designation, showing the grace of our Lord Jesus in His incarnation.

Indwelt by the Spirit of God for his ministry (Ezekiel 2:2), Ezekiel was inspired to preach to his own people whether or not they would pay attention. Like the Saviour of whom he spoke he must devour the word given to him (Ezekiel 2:9-3:1). Ezekiel knew full well that what lay ahead of Israel and of him in some measure contained lamentations, mourning and woe; Christ knew that those three would be borne by Himself. As suggested by his name, Ezekiel must face and outface, with a forehead like adamant harder than flint, an impudent and hard-hearted generation. How desperately sad that the people of God should ever be thus described! How gracious was God to provide a faithful outline of His will, purposes and mercy to them!

So consequent was the ministry entrusted to Ezekiel that had he not fulfilled it, in spite of his being surrounded by 'briars, thorns and scorpions', he would be held responsible for that rebellious house to whom he preached; he was God's watchman; he must give them warning! That warning must also be to the righteous, that they might not discard their righteous ways. Perspective for his task was given by a double vision of God's glory (Ezekiel 1:28; 3:23); his message and motivation were provided by the hand of God (Ezekiel 2:8; 3:11); his destination and ministry were at the direction and movement of the Spirit of God (Ezekiel 3:14); and his physical restraints, like those of Paul, were imposed on him along with the grace to succeed under them (Ezekiel 3:26,27). As the Saviour of whom he bore witness (Acts 10:43) and as servants of God today for whom he is an example, he must speak only those things that were delivered to him. To be an accurate channel of divine revelation he must listen carefully and personally take to heart everything God said irrespective of audience response.

Like that of all servants of God, the task was daunting; the help was sure. Nowhere in the book is any hint that Ezekiel even hesitated to fully proclaim God's message. What is recorded is significant: he came to where the people were and sat among them, overwhelmed. The revelation of the likeness of God must balance his appreciation of the plight of the people, the one not skewing the other. Then Ezekiel was ready for his task. The glory that appeared to Ezekiel at his commission (Ezekiel 3:23) was like that that he had seen by the River Chebar. What glory was that? The appearance of the likeness of the glory of the LORD (Ezekiel 1:28). Its effect was worship: he fell on his face. A true vision of God, though veiled, as it must be, will surely have the same effect on all who would serve Him.

What, then, are the lessons for us from the introduction to Ezekiel and his calling? God's judgement on Judah began when King Josiah tried to stop Pharaoh Neco on his way to Carchemish. (Israel's (the northern kingdom's) captivity had occurred much earlier). Eight years later Ezekiel was carried away, and eleven years later Jerusalem fell. God's time, not ours, is what the universe runs on, and God's judgements are sure. Had it not been for the sacrifice of Christ at the fullness of the time we all would have perished. A vision of God's glory is essential to all of us, coming no longer in dreams and visions, but in the Word of God, the Scriptures (Luke 24:27); it was clearly demonstrated before the commission of Isaiah (6), Jeremiah (1) and Ezekiel. It resulted firstly in worship and then the willingness to serve. At thirty, Ezekiel in other circumstances would have entered his priestly duties; at thirty he certainly was called to his prophetic ones; long before that God was preparing him. We each must factor our own age and experience into the equation. God is able to prepare and use the youngest!

When God told Ezekiel to stand, he was enabled to do so by the Holy Spirit. Our ability will be likewise accomplished. The rebellion of others in their obstinacy and stubbornness, mentioned sixteen times in Ezekiel, eight in his commission, is to be no deterrent to obedience to the call of God. He was to preach whether they heard or not. Ezekiel uses the title 'sovereign LORD' 217 times in this book. A faithful servant must never question God's right to exercise His sovereign will. God's word was to Ezekiel as the sweetness of honey. The sweetness that the messenger tastes comes from the Sender of the message; although sometimes the content of the message itself must of necessity be less than appealing.

3

EZEKIEL'S VISIONS OF GOD

Ezekiel's ministry was to be a difficult one. Already Israel had been carried away by Assyria, and now the flower of Judah's nobility had been taken captive into Babylonia. Yet Judah took no warning to cleanse their ways. Instead, they steeped themselves more deeply in their idolatries and vices, a true fulfilment of Jeremiah's prophecy (chapter 24) about the good and bad figs: the ones that were left in the land and shortly to be taken were very bad indeed. All, in the land and in Babylonia, believed that they were impervious to God's judgement through Nebuchadnezzar – in spite of Jeremiah's teaching. To preach to such required special strengthening, and that was given by the heavens being opened and visions of God being given to God's servant.

Three things are evident in the vision that Ezekiel saw: What is seen is only the appearance of the likeness of what is represented. The primary vision is one of fearful impending judgement coming from the north, from Babylon. And the intricacy of the lower part of the actual vision, the living creatures and wheels, stands in contrast to the vagueness of what is represented as seen in the likeness of the appearance of the One who inhabits the likeness of the throne that stands above it all. That part of the vision is purposely hidden. No man can see God and live (Exodus 33:20). He is the One whom no one has seen nor can see (1 Timothy 6:16).

Physical shapes here represent Him so that Ezekiel could behold Him at all. Thank God that the Old Testament representation of the likeness of Him has been far superseded by the New! The only begotten Son who is in the bosom of the Father, He has 'exegeted' Him, told Him forth (John 1:18). He is the fullness of the glory of God, the impress image of His substance (Hebrews 1:3). "He who has seen me has seen the Father" (John 14:9). Christ incarnate and Christ revealed through the Word form the prism through which the believer can behold the blinding light of heaven. We see the light of the knowledge of the glory of God shining in the face of Christ (2 Corinthians 4:6). But first and foremost in Ezekiel's vision God is viewed as a God of righteous judgement. Flashes of fire whirl and catch each other in a lightning-swift whirlwind as the vision approaches from the north. And from the midst of the inferno there is an amber glowing like the glowing of molten metal - the presence of the Lord.

Yet His presence is at first detected in His servants. Their character is representative of Him. It is through the clear delineation of them that we behold something of the One whom they serve. The likeness of the Master should always be clearly depicted in the character of the servant (Matthew 10:25). Cherubim are living spirit beings, without physical bodies which our eyes can detect. They obviously are not equipped with the visible members that physical bodies possess: hands, feet, heads and wings. These are words, symbols used to represent the character of those holy beings that inhabit eternity, symbols so that we can picture in our feeble minds what is unseen by our eyes. What, then, can we take from Ezekiel's vision?

Four living creatures, each with four faces, four wings, four hands, are called cherubim in Ezekiel 10. Cherubim appeared in Eden, guarding the way to the tree of life; they are represented again in the book of Revelation (e.g. chapter 4) in the midst of and guarding the throne of heaven. So careful is Ezekiel to let us know that their depiction is only a likeness that he uses the expression fifteen times. First, each had four faces - the face of a lion, an ox, a man and an eagle, perhaps signifying that each had strength, an ability to serve, intelligence and a heavenly character. Seemingly, though hard to visualize, each could see in every direction with each face, a clear picture of the all-knowing character of the One whom they represent and serve. The wings and hands show their ability to fully serve.

They moved directly forward, never turning, shadow-less in the prosecution of the will of their God. Like burning coals of fire they illustrated the holiness of God; their swiftness to do His will is seen in their flashing to and fro like lightning. The wings of each of the four are joined together, demonstrating the unity so delightful to God (Psalm 133), and the sound of their movements is like the sound of many waters, like the sound of the voice of God Almighty. The cherubim fully demonstrate the attributes of the servant of God as well as those of God Himself. The marvel of it all is that God also allows us to serve, who fall so far short in every direction! It is noteworthy that the character of Christ who is the image of God is likewise seen in the fourfold face represented by the writers of the four Gospels: Matthew, the Lion, the King; Mark, the Ox, the Servant; Luke, the Man, the Intelligence; and John, the Eagle, the One who soars above the heavens, the Son of God.

Beside each of the cherubs stood a wheel on the earth (Ezekiel 1:15), a wheel whose rim, whose height, was high and lofty, unswerving wheels within wheels moving with the balance and surety of gyroscopes, wheels full of eyes round about, wheels keeping pace with the living creatures, led by the Spirit. These were able to move forward in any direction without turning, whirling in tremendous rapidity. And the whole, a representation of the omniscience of God, governed what must happen on the earth. In the immediate situation there was to be divine judgement on Judah. The things on earth merely shadowed things going on in the heavens, as both Daniel 10:13ff and Ephesians 6:12 clearly demonstrate. Running to and fro on earth, the wheels move with heavenly power, wheels of divine government, all-seeing, all-powerful through the Spirit of the living creatures within them.

Above and beyond the vision of cherubim and corresponding wheels is the structure above in the firmament, and from there issues a voice that causes the movement of the wings of the cherubim to cease. God speaks; let all else be still and listen! There, on the likeness of a sapphire throne, sits the likeness of a man, a likeness wreathed in fire with a central glow of molten metal described as amber, and around about a brightness of unapproachable holiness and glory. This is the likeness of the appearance of the glory of the Almighty. Ezekiel, recognizing it for what it is, says, "I fell on my face." Could any demonstration of the glory of the LORD cause any other human reaction? Would that we were more often on our faces beholding the divine revelation in our own day!

But there was something else that Ezekiel and we must see in connection with the judgement to follow, something most essential for his preparation to be a servant and prophet of the Lord and ours to appreciate. The appearance of the radiance of majesty around about the throne was the appearance of a rainbow that appears in the clouds on a rainy day. This was the likeness of the glory of the Lord. Well might the realization that the fearful judgement of God was tinged with all that the rainbow on a rainy day represents (Genesis 9:13ff) cause worship on Ezekiel's part and on ours who have seen the mercy of God so clearly surrounding the whole indescribable judgement of Calvary.

Ezekiel had to learn, as do we, that as this world deteriorates into conditions predicted for the last days, when "some will fall away from the faith" (1 Timothy 4:1), when difficult times will come when men will be "lovers of self, lovers of money, boastful, arrogant, revilers ... lovers of pleasure rather than lovers of God" (2 Timothy 3:1-4), that there is above and beyond all the throne of One who is in complete control, and about that throne is the radiance of a rainbow in the day of rain! The merciful character of God shines through all His judgements.

We live in a day of events that stagger, of natural catastrophe of Biblical proportion, of weaponry and evil that when combined might easily shatter the peace of heart we have in Christ, when consummate evil and its expression have reached unparalleled depths. God's city of the future will be called, "The LORD is there." God's people of today should rest in a similar realization. In the place to which God has called and brought us, Jehovah shammah, the Lord is there!

4

EZEKIEL'S IMAGERY AND SYMBOLISM

Ezekiel, directed by the Spirit of God, used nearly every possible literary method of reaching the people of Judah with whom he was in captivity. They were a people who preferred lies to the truth, who would not accept the inevitability of Jerusalem's overthrow and their own lengthy exile. Symbolism and imagery were among the most widely utilized of those methods; Ezekiel himself was to be mute.

A brick, an iron plate, cakes baked over cows' dung, a razor, a cross on the forehead, baggage, a battle axe, a sword, a cauldron, a flowing river, a valley full of dry bones, a couple of sticks - the book seems full of object lessons, concrete examples of the mind of God outlined in detail for an obstinate people. Our purpose is spiritual rather than literary, but the technique is interesting nonetheless. To their shame and sorrow the general population of Judah was unreceptive no matter what the presentation. Ezekiel was "to them like a sensual song by one who has a beautiful voice and plays well on an instrument; for they hear your words, but they do not practice them" (Ezekiel 33:32).

To their sorrow, unheeded warnings resulted in the lamentations, mourning and woe that God had shown Ezekiel the people would have to bear. By the fulfilment of his prophecies they would know that a prophet had been in their midst (Ezekiel 33:33). There were ten of these object lessons that applied before Jerusalem was sacked. We'll examine some of these in more detail in a future chapter, but look at them now briefly, what they should have meant to the captives and what we can learn for ourselves.

Ezekiel was to be generally struck dumb, albeit able to speak when God spoke, for four and a half years until Jerusalem fell (Ezekiel 3:26,27; 24:27), but the actions of his life must be an epistle, known and read by all, and that very fact is a strong lesson about our own lives and deeds. Actions often speak even louder than words. Christ is the brilliant example of one who went about doing good: even "Christ did not please Himself" (John 5:20; 8:29; Romans 15:3). Ezekiel's first sign was at great discomfort to himself (chapter 4), as were some that followed, a clear indication that the way of the servant of God, like the way of the transgressor, can be hard. The end is not yet. If in the world we have tribulation, the time is fast approaching when He will manifest Himself who has overcome the world (John 16:33). Lying restrained on one side and then the other each day for well over a year had to bring all its own pain, to say nothing of disruption to his normal life. There was little to comfort save the knowledge that he was being obedient to his God. (Paul speaks of being comforted in his own hardships (2 Corinthians 1:3,4); personal comfort, however, is not granted to make us comfortable, but to make us comforters.) Personal discomfort, even anguish, borne submissively can be a striking testimony in itself (Ezekiel 12:9; 24:19).

2 Corinthians 11:23ff further exemplifies the point that as servants of the Lord we may suffer hardship. Not only must Ezekiel's suffering be physical, but emotional as well (Ezekiel 4:14), and the total amount of

food offered was about eight ounces of bread and two-thirds of a quart of water per day. All this was to be prepared by himself with only a fire of cows' dung to help. Obvious in the sign was an impending shortage of food. Its baking procedure, though Ezekiel achieved some reprieve in the matter of cleanliness, indicated defilement in the foods of the nations to which Israel would be driven - a fact that Daniel and his friends ran into even in high places (Daniel 1:8). But if God's provision for us, though seemingly meagre, accomplishes His purposes, should we not be satisfied? He has promised not to forget us in our need.

A sharp sword shaving the hair of Ezekiel's head and beard must have cut a man groomed for the priesthood very deeply (Leviticus 19:27; 21:5). But in Ezekiel 5 the shaving was as much a testimony to errant Israel as the hair of the head had been to the nation when more obedient. A sword, rather than a razor, would teach the observers of the sword that would bring about their disaster in the hands of the Chaldeans. A third of the hair burnt in the city indicated the population who would be consumed with famine. A third was to be scattered to the winds. Fewer than a third of the people would survive even to the captivity, and only a very few become a preserved remnant in the eventual return to the land. The people heard, but did not believe. Ezekiel's message must go forth anyway, "whether they listen or not" (Ezekiel 2:5,7; 3:11).

Chapter 12 provides Ezekiel with further discomfort. He must pack his belongings by day, so that all may see what he is about. Previous captivity would have ensured that they understood Ezekiel's inference. Then he must dig through the wall with his hands as night fell upon him and with hidden and unseeing face depart as though into exile. His explanation to the people described how King Zedekiah would try to escape, be caught, and go blinded into his captivity and imprisonment (2 Kings 25:1-7; Jeremiah 52:4-11). The prophet must also eat and drink in front of the people with a tremor in his hand and anxiety upon his face just as those in Jerusalem and Judah would do. His every action must show what his belief was concerning the fulfilment of the promises of God. Ezekiel is not only a sign to the people of Israel, he is an example to servants of God in every generation!

Whitewashing walls when they should have been thoroughly prepared, mortared, established, only invites disaster when the floods come (Ezekiel 13:10-14). This lesson described the action of the false prophets who could only envision and speak of peace in a world bound for judgement, and speaks loudly to God's people today as well. This poor old world will not 'every day in every way get better and better' (2 Timothy 3:1-4)! To live as though it were permanent and the thing that is our greatest treasure, would be every bit as wrong as the false prophecies of old.

Somewhere along the line Ezekiel took to himself a wife. We don't often think of his life as portraying a man in loving relationship, but the testimony of God concerning him, as siege was laid to Jerusalem and that great city began to fall, bore beautiful witness to a successful marriage. In spite of the stringencies of captivity, in spite of idiosyncrasies of a man whose life was impacted by his desire to accomplish the will of God for him, the upset to house and home, the upset to a "normal" home life, God describes in Ezekiel the secret of a happy marriage. His wife was "the desire of your eyes" (Ezekiel 24:16). He was to lose even her to the will of the LORD. What is more, mourning and tears were not to be apparent. His groaning must be internal only; his demeanour must not betray the loss of the affection that he had cherished. His actions would demonstrate what would follow to the inhabitants of Jerusalem; they would rot away in their iniquities, and they would groan to one another. As Ezekiel had done, so they would do, that the nation would know that

God was Lord (Ezekiel 24:24). Ah, that our actions might demonstrate the same! The sign that followed, that the dumb man spoke, would also show that God was Lord (Ezekiel 24:27).

Once the fall of Jerusalem was accomplished and reported, once those already in captivity realized that Ezekiel's message had been true, God began to reveal something of future blessings in restoration. There was only one sign sermon shown in the book that portrayed something of the restoration of the nation. Ezekiel 37:16ff instructs the prophet to take two sticks illustrative of Judah and Joseph, write their names upon them, and join them into one stick as a sign of future blessing and unity (see also Hosea 1:11). When Israel was brought into existence in 1947, Ezekiel 37 was the scripture that David Ben Gurion, the Prime Minister, used, but there is to be a still fuller fulfilment to the prophecy. David, their ancient king, will again be their prince and their shepherd. God will be their God. God's promise to David of one forever sitting upon his throne and to Israel of eternal forgiveness and blessing will shortly come to pass. Interspersed with these sign lessons were direct prophecies, visions and parables lending conviction to the message.

5

EZEKIEL'S VISIONS

As well as the vision that Ezekiel describes in chapter one: a whirling storm cloud enfolding itself and containing various beings and wheels full of eyes, all prophesying judgement and revealing something of the character of God and divine government; there were other visions, parables, direct prophecies all to do with Jerusalem's fall, judgement on other nations and eventual restoration and forgiveness. That first vision is repeated in chapter 10 with some variations and further lessons. A second multi-faceted vision occurs some five years before the fall of Jerusalem and runs through chapters 8 to 11. It investigates in some detail the sins of Jerusalem and the Lord's departure from the house of God and the holy city.

The third vision, again with many facets, is that of a restored nation, priesthood, offerings, temple, city and land. It occurs between chapter 40 and the end of the book. It pictures millennial glory and the transcending majesty of the One who will reign, the never-ending glory of the city whose God is in her midst, and the blessings that will flow in abundance - all of which would have been applied to Israel all the way through had they but shown the obedience and trust demanded of them.

What was unable to be accomplished through the disobedience of the many will surely be accomplished through the obedience of the One and the fruits of His work at Calvary.

Quickly reviewing the vision of chapter one with the additional comments of chapter ten, we see the likeness of God upon His throne calling for the dispensing of judgement, the scattering of coals from between the cherubim (Ezekiel 1:13; 10:2) over the sinning city. The prominence of the eyes covering the bodies, backs, hands, wings and wheels leads us to realize the omniscience, the all-knowing character of the God of heaven who was seated above the cherubim. There is nothing that He does not see and know. Revelation 4:8 also envisions creatures full of eyes surrounding the throne of God. If this is the description of perfect servants of God, should it not be incumbent on imperfect humans who also seek to serve? Not only are eyes round about important. Eyes within sensing sin, weakness, failure, all leading to confession and purity are necessary. One of the faces of the cherubim was described as the face of a cherub here in chapter 10, the face of an ox in chapter 1. This may have been a copyist's error, or a cherub's face may have resembled an ox. We recall that this is only an appearance of the likeness of something spiritual without the form of either.

High and lofty wheels that had stood firmly on the earth now whirled, moved and rose, the beginning of the departure of the divine presence from the house of God. The slow movement from place to place by creatures that bore the throne of His glory that might have moved as flashes of lightning rather indicate the reluctance of God to leave His temple, the patience that so often works even in our own weaknesses. As His glory departed, 'Ichabod' might have been again written over Jerusalem. It is interesting to map out the departure: from the threshold of the house to the east gate, over the Kidron Valley to the Mount of

Olives - the journey really prefigured another to be enacted some 500 years later when the Divine Son left the house, left the city, left the earth. But He was to return in the Person of the Holy Spirit ten days later that you and I might know His presence, both in our personal lives and in God's House.

About five years prior to Jerusalem's overthrow (Ezekiel 8:1), Ezekiel in a vision is taken to Jerusalem where he is shown one of the reasons for the dire judgement to follow: God would not permit Himself to dwell with an image of jealousy, an idol set up within the limits of the temple. The very first commandment of God forbade such arrant idolatry. The vision reveals still more nefarious activities. Among the elderhood exists a secret cult of seventy who offer up incense to gods that are depicted as beasts and detestable creeping things intermingled with personal idols. Then he sees women weeping for Tammuz in his supposed death, rejoicing at his supposed resurrection. Then twenty-five sun worshippers are seen standing between the altar and the front porch of the house, facing away from God to the east instead of the west.

These were no doubt priests because they stood in the court of the priests. The whole temple scene was one of corruption and apostasy, and in hand with it violence filling the land that should have been exuding peace. When God's house is defiled, as is seen also in the churches in Revelation 2 and 3, when time for repentance is past, there is no place for God. He must leave and the house now desolate faces sure destruction. Chapter nine gives us the picture of the destruction.

Six city guards, who we suggest were angels, and a man dressed in linen with a scribe's case of pens and ink enter the city: the man to mark with a cross the foreheads of those whose sighs and tears demonstrated that their hearts were in line with the Lord's, the angels to dispense the judgement to all who weren't so marked. Beginning at the sanctuary the man and angels fulfilled their task. At the end of it, Ezekiel alone was standing, causing Ezekiel to exclaim at the destruction to be fulfilled. Ezekiel pleaded for the nation to which he prophesied, and was in this a good example for us who are ministering to a sinning world. But the sin had gone too far. God will not always plead with man. Sooner or later He will dispense the judgement deserved. Our task is to pray and preach! Then we must thank God for the grace that allowed the mark of the cross to be on our foreheads. Thanks be to God that we belong to Christ! Then follows chapter 10 with the departure of the glory to which we have referred.

We then skip to Ezekiel's third vision (chapters 40 to 48), a future city, a future temple, a purified priesthood who will do all God's will, a land of Israel revised and reorganized, a land to glorify the Lord who will be there. If the measurements given are to be taken literally, and if the river that flows from the presence of God is to flow as described (Ezekiel 47:1-12), some tremendous topographical changes are to take place at the coming back to earth of the Lord Jesus. We know from other scriptures that that will be so (e.g. Zechariah 14:4,10). Whether they will be sufficient to accommodate all Ezekiel's measurements or whether some of them are in some way symbolic we will have to leave for the moment, but will revisit the problem in a future chapter.

However, for your thought meantime, the Jordan River would have to be removed some miles to the east to accommodate the seemingly newly situated city of Jerusalem and the portion of the prince and surrounding areas. The river that flows from the presence of God and His house would have to flow upwards to get to the Dead Sea. Nothing is impossible with God, of course, but there may be some presently hidden symbolism seen in Ezekiel's vision. These things do, after all, appear in a vision, and the two previous visions are largely symbolic as we have seen. These are things we can wonder at at leisure, but there are matters we can understand that will provide ample lessons for us meantime.

In spite of topographical questions, the river that flows at varying depths and brings such purity and healing wherever it goes, seems physical rather than simply symbolic, and is a continuing example of the presence and blessing of the LORD. Zechariah (Zechariah 14:8) afterwards tells us that the river will flow west to the Mediterranean as well as east to the Jordan. Joel (Joel 3:18) predates Ezekiel in his mention also of that river. As with all blessings, whether physical or spiritual, that flow from the presence of God, they grow as they go, bringing life to the dead and supporting life everywhere that they touch. Even the Dead Sea, six times saltier than the ocean, will spring to life, fresh from the presence of God. One can stand to the side of divine blessing, and like the fishermen cast nets and reap bounty. The angelic messenger led Ezekiel right through the river; water to swim in invite us to experience yet greater depths of the blessings of God, not only in sweet millennial days, but in the present.

6

OF HIM ALL THE PROPHETS BEAR WITNESS

Lest we become mesmerized with the vast variety of the depiction of things and places in Ezekiel's book, we need to remind ourselves that he also portrays the Lord Jesus Christ, as did all the prophets (Acts 10:43), as did all the Scriptures (Luke 24:27). Some prophets, like Jonah, became a sign; some like Isaiah, spoke direct prophecies; some, like Ezekiel saw visions and told parables that exalted Christ. A brief examination of some things that Ezekiel saw and did and said will teach us something or at least remind us of what God sees in His Holy Servant, His well-beloved Son.

Ezekiel begins his book as he did his ministry with the heavens being opened and seeing the appearance of the likeness of God in various visions. Perfect servants depicted in the symbolic likeness of the form of cherubim along with their mysterious wheels became the chariot of the One seated on a throne above them in his vision. God, who needs none to support or transport, in grace uses His servants to participate in His actions. Their bodies were perfectly suited to their calling and displayed their abilities. As servants of God they must reflect the likeness of the

One they served. Their four faces depicted four characteristics of Christ also seen by the Gospel writers in their New Testament books: Matthew writes of Christ the King, seen in the face of the stately lion in Ezekiel's vision; Mark portrays the Serving Christ, seen in the face of ox or cherub; Luke, Christ the Man as portrayed in the face of the man seen by the prophet; John, the Son of God, as depicted by Ezekiel's eagle.

These four 'faces' of Christ are again seen as the various prophets declare Him to be the branch from the stem of Jesse, the royal line (Isaiah 11:1), "My servant the Branch" (Zechariah 3:8), "Behold, a man whose name is Branch" (Zechariah 6:12), and "in that day the Branch of the LORD will be beautiful and glorious," the Son of God (Isaiah 4:2). We marvel as we meditate on Ezekiel's words: 'and this was their appearance: they had human form' (Ezekiel 1:5). That the same should ever have been said concerning Christ (Philippians 2:7) and that He should retain that in heaven today, the Man upon the throne, is even more astounding than the mysterious visions of the likeness of God in Ezekiel's book. That man on earth can likewise exemplify Christ is equally astounding. Ezekiel himself becomes a picture of Christ in some of the things reported of him and in some of his object lessons to guilty Israel.

He was carried about by the Spirit (Ezekiel 3:14; Matthew 4:1); he came to where the captives sat and sat there (Ezekiel 3:15; John 1:11); he was obedient to every call of God (Ezekiel 12:7; Philippians 2:8), eating the scroll written front and back with lamentations, mourning and woe, reminding us of the Man of Sorrows whose life progressed with strong crying and tears. Christ, like Ezekiel, knew the sweetness of the word as He consumed it; like John (Revelation 10:9,10). He knew the bitterness that the word would bring to Him as He fulfilled it. Being made a watchman to iniquitous men, their blood required at his hand, lying bound as with ropes, unable to move save in obedience to the commands of God and mute save for the words that the Lord gave him to speak, and bearing the iniquity of those who passed disinterestedly by - the whole picture of Ezekiel's life seemed to be a reliving of Isaiah 53, a picture of the life and suffering of Christ.

Judah would see his sorrows; "As for you, son of man, groan with breaking heart and bitter grief, groan in their sight" (Ezekiel 21:6,7). "Cry out and wail, son of man" is a preview of the Lord's descent from the top of Olivet, mourning over what might have been in Jerusalem, "Jerusalem, Jerusalem, ... How often I wanted to gather ... and you were unwilling" (Matthew 23:37)!

Then in chapter five a sharp sword must again take the measure of Jerusalem's judgement and dispersal. Ezekiel's shaving sword was the same word that he used 83 times in the book for the sword used mostly in judgement. His hair removal portrayed the city's destruction. A third of the hair was to be burnt, a third smitten with the sword, a third scattered to the winds and chased by the sword, and only a few bound in one of the edges of Ezekiel's robes for safekeeping. The eradication of Judah's pernicious idolatry, its high places, its apostasy, would shortly bring the fire and sword to her. Only a very few inhabitants would eventually be spared, and that only because of the tender mercy of God. Ezekiel clapped his hands as ordered by God, not in pleasure but in derision, to make the people know that God is the Lord, the only One to be worshipped, the supreme authority. Christ, like Ezekiel, took the measure of sins, only this time of the world. The sword instead of shaving Him was plunged into His bosom (Zechariah 13:7). Unlike Ezekiel who saw so little of blessing, He shall see of the travail of His soul and be satisfied (Isaiah 53:11).

There were some in the land who actually believed Ezekiel's prophecies.

They just couldn't convince themselves of an early fulfilment (Ezekiel 12:27). Satan has three great lies: there is no heaven; there is no hell; there is no hurry! The last one may claim more souls than the other two, and also affect believers in their service. Peter, speaking seriously about the consummation of the age prescribes urgency to all; although the Lord is longsuffering, not wishing any to perish, but all to come to repentance, the time is at hand (2 Peter 3:3-10)!

On the day that Nebuchadnezzar began the final siege of Jerusalem, Ezekiel proclaimed a parable to the captives in Babylonia. It was on the tenth of the tenth month. The number ten is so often associated with judgement in Scripture. A large pot made of bronze (also associated with judgement) with water poured into it was put on a pile of flaming wood so that the water might boil vigorously (Ezekiel 24:6-11). Into the water were put choice cuts of lamb and the bones and spices. The whole would be consumed or removed, the bones burned, and still the pot would be heated until the bronze glowed in the heat. The pot and contents depicted Jerusalem and inhabitants. Their rust must be consumed in the flaming fervency.

The lesson of complete destruction was evident. But think for a moment of the One who some five hundred years later bore Jerusalem's judgement and that of the world, the Lamb whose bones were afflicted with fire from on high (Lamentations 1:13), when He who could suffer infinitely was judged infinitely. There was no rust on His part to be consumed. Satan had nothing in Him. Our own hearts are consumed with joy mingled with sorrow and appreciation as we try to enter into the scene. This scene with the pot was followed by the sudden announcement of the taking away of the desire of Ezekiel's life, his wife, with a blow (Ezekiel 24:16). One shudders at the pain of one doing such good and yet bearing such sorrow. "Look and see if there is any pain like my pain which was severely dealt out to me ..." (Lamentations 1:12). "Remember my affliction and my wandering, the wormwood and bitterness" (Lamentations 3:19). All this was done so that Israel might know "... when it comes then you will know that I am the LORD GOD" (Ezekiel 24:24).

The vision of the valley of dry bones has often been used as a lesson in Gospel preaching. As in creation (Genesis 2:7) the breath of God alone could bring life, and Ezekiel's vision of bleached, dry bones scattered through a huge valley, speaking of the condition of Israel, needed that breath to bring back life. Ezekiel was the instrument used to bring the breath through his prophecy (Ezekiel 37:10). The bones, unburied, and that in itself an abomination, then came together, bone to its bone; muscle and flesh followed and then the bones stood and lived. The vision illustrated what God could and would do to Israel to restore their place and glory in times yet future (Jeremiah 31:33; 33:14-16; Matthew 24:30,31). Linked with this vision was a picture of Israel as two sticks, sticks that should be united into one, never to be separated again. These will be together under one shepherd, David. But none of this could be accomplished apart from the King who will reign, the King whom Israel rejected, but who will be received and worshipped in that future day.

7

GOD'S JUDGEMENT ON JUDAH AND JERUSALEM

The ten tribes of northern Israel had been carried away and dispersed by Assyria about 125 years by the time Ezekiel prophesied. Because the southern kingdom of Judah had not learned from the sins of the northern kingdom but had perpetuated them in spite of continuous warnings and instruction she, too, was about to fall. Two incursions by Nebuchadnezzar had carried away much of Judah's nobility and riches, including Daniel and Ezekiel.

Ezekiel prophesied to those already in captivity, although his messages concern Jerusalem's downfall and the destruction of neighbouring nations condemned because of their attitudes to God's house and God's people. Besides clear sign lessons such as the iron plate set against the depicted city with its sign concerning the scarcity of bread in chapter 4, the applying of the sword to the hair of his head and body in chapter 5, direct prophecies concerning the idolatrous cause of judgement in chapter 6 and warnings about the severity of Jerusalem's judgement in chapter 7, there were prophecies through visions told in chapters 8 to 11 and parables in chapters 15-17, 23 and 24. In the direct prophecies alone the word comes seven times in some form: "Then you will know that I am the LORD."

The visions include a visionary visit to Jerusalem to the temple, the House of God, exposing the sin and degradation that impelled severe judgement. At the north gate of the temple Ezekiel saw an idol that provoked the jealousy of God standing next to the altar gate (Ezekiel 8:5). Greater abominations than this breaking of the first commandment were to be revealed. At the entrance of the court where the elders of Judah worshipped, were carved all the idols of Israel replete with creeping things, detestable beasts and other abominations (Ezekiel 8:10), and in front of them the seventy elders offering incense to them. Worse yet, at the gate of the Lord's house the women wept for the rites of spring, the death and resurrection of Tammuz complete with its base immorality (Ezekiel 8:14). Greater abominations than these were to be revealed, for the higher the position of those involved and their nearness to the inner courts of God's house, the greater the responsibility, the greater the sin. Twenty-five priests (were these the high priest and the twenty-four leaders of song?) with their backs to the LORD and facing the rising sun were worshipping the creation rather than the Creator (Ezekiel 8:16). His eye would have no pity on them in their coming distress. Their prayers would go unheeded and there would come no pity. In that age or in any other, man cannot with impunity play fast and loose with the revealed commandments of God. The greater the position of responsibility, the greater the deserved judgement, not only on those directly involved, but on all the people. The glory of God must depart from such a people.

Judah and Israel are then described in some basic and earthy language, a parable of an adulterous woman (Ezekiel 16). Jerusalem, the city not the people, had its origin with the Jebusites, which may have been closely associated with Amorites and Hittites. Like a newborn unattended and left to die, pagan Jerusalem wallowed in blood, but under David's leadership at God's command she began to live and thrive. God set His house there; she became His. He brought her to maturity. Her beauty became legendary, magnificent, queenly. But as a prostitute Jerusalem forgot the One who loved her and set His name upon her.

She set herself after strange gods and abominable practices. Idols and high places, even child sacrifice (Ezekiel 16:21,22), consumed her interests. Judgement would of necessity consume her beauty, her pride and boasting, her people. The analogy goes on and on. All the characteristics that had applied to the people who were part of her origin were seen in her (Ezekiel 16:44) and we wonder at her degeneration, unmindful perhaps that if we let Satan have any part of his way among God's elect today the analogy would apply to us as well.

Ezekiel continues, linking her with Samaria and Sodom, both of whom had been steeped in degradation, both of whom had fallen under the supreme judgement of God. Solomon for his day (Proverbs 26:11), Peter for ours (2 Peter 2:22), rightly describe one who would despise such goodness of God and resort to the works of the flesh as dogs returning to their own vomit. Both of these men write by the Spirit of God! Yet in spite of God's distaste for the folly of Judah and His determination to punish sin as He must, He still found room in His heart for forgiveness on the basis of repentance and atonement (Ezekiel 16:61). His mercy would restore a remnant; its fullness would materialize in a day yet future.

Ezekiel is then told to pose a riddle (the Hebrew word is 'hidah' – which is the same word that is used in Judges 14:12 and 1 Kings 10:1), one given in chapter Ezekiel 17:1-3 and explained in Ezekiel 11-21. Nebuchadnezzar would continue his attacks on Jerusalem, but once again in the middle of judgement God remembers mercy. The city would immediately fall, but it would be revived in a day yet future, a kingdom that will produce branches and bear fruit in millennial times under a King from David's line. This will be a kingdom that rules the whole world (Daniel 2:44; Zechariah 14:3ff).

Glorious days lie ahead for Israel, not because of her actions, but because of the promises of God made possible through Israel's Messiah at Calvary. Chapter 18 sets straight the misguided thought that people were to be punished for the sins of others. While individuals might be adversely affected by others' transgressions, there remains individual responsibility to God for behaviour. Individual repentance is required (Ezekiel 18:30). God has no pleasure in the death of the unrighteous, but pleads yet for due repentance (Ezekiel 18:32). Kingly position was no reason for sparing judgement as the lamentation of chapter 19 over Jehoahaz who was taken captive by Pharaoh Neco to Egypt (2 Kings 23:33), and Jehoiachin who was taken to Babylon by Nebuchadnezzar (2 Kings 24:15) clearly shows. Indeed, position brings more responsibility and corresponding judgement (James 3:1), both then and now.

Several chapters follow in which God refuses to answer the cries of Israel's elders, citing a long list of the nation's rejecting of Him. The day of judgement had come and God speaks of that in several analogies: God's sword was drawn to smite, a sword sharpened and polished to make slaughter, one that would flash like lightning. His sword would be made bare in the sword of Babylon's king. God would overrule in the omens that Nebuchadnezzar questioned. Jerusalem was next! As well as the picture of death by the sword, Israel, because of her bloodshed, would be melted in a crucible, a furnace of such affliction that her dross might be purged. The elders and priests had not distinguished between the holy and the profane, the clean and the unclean, and were given to dishonest gain (Ezekiel 22:26-29). Now the furnace of divine affliction would consume Jerusalem. We cannot read such chapters without asking ourselves how clearly we distinguish between the holy and profane, between the clean and unclean.

God then gave Ezekiel and us a parable of two sisters and called them Oholah and Oholibah. Both names come from 'ohel' the Hebrew word for 'tent'. Oholah means 'her tent' and may describe her actions with regards worship. The sanctuaries within her were her own doing. Oholibah means, 'my tent is in her' and rather describes God's dwelling at Jerusalem. Oholah, the northern kingdom, lusted after Assyria and was subsequently delivered into their hands. But Oholibah, the southern kingdom, defiled herself being more corrupt in her lust than her sister and unwarned by her demise. Lusting after Chaldea rather than appreciating God's house in her midst would result in her being delivered completely into Babylon's hands (Ezekiel 23:23,24).

Perhaps the thing that affects us most deeply is the realization that the fearful judgement of an angry God could be seen in many of the same terms, carried out for the sinfulness of mankind upon the righteous Son of God at Calvary. He bore God's sword, God's fire, God's melting to complete consumption as fire from on high entered into His bones, and we bow in wonder, love and praise.

8

GOD'S JUDGEMENT OF THE NATIONS

After the final siege of Jerusalem had actually begun and before he spoke at length about the glory days of Israel that shall yet be, Ezekiel turned his prophecies against Israel's neighbouring countries. Seven nations were included: Ammon, Moab and Edom on the east, Philistia on the west, Tyre and Sidon on the north, and Egypt on the south. While Ezekiel prophesied to, and his messages were directed to, the captivity of Judah in Babylon principally for their benefit, his messages from God included these surrounding nations, whether or not they were delivered to them. Those who blessed the descendants of Abraham were to be blessed; those who cursed them would also be cursed (Genesis 12:1-3). Ezekiel chapters 25-32 deal with these judgements and included among them was judgement against Satan who motivated them.

David had previously conquered Ammon, but after Solomon's death that nation had regained their strength and recommenced hostility with Israel. In hopes of getting additional territory Ammon sided with Nebuchadnezzar (2 Kings 24:1,2) and then later sided with Judah against Babylon. Nebuchadnezzar had commenced his attack on Tyre (its defeat took 13 years, largely because of her navy) and then had to decide between

Ammon and Judah. In God's overruling he was directed to attack Judah. Her time had come. Again hoping to profit from Judah's demise, Ammon rejoiced at her defeat. Because of her attitude Ammon would be overrun by eastern nomads who would completely cut her off, reducing even Ammon's capital to a stable for camels (Ezekiel 25:5).

Moab was to be overrun by the same tribes that destroyed Ammon and for similar reasons. Moab had been at odds with Israel most of the time since Balak, its king, hired Balaam to curse her. While David had conquered her for the length of his reign and the reign of Solomon, she again revolted, treating Judah and Judah's God with contempt, making Jerusalem out to be just like all other nations, denying that her God had given her any special treatment. Envy and contempt against the people of God is hardly blessing. God's judgement must fall on Moab and the Mount Seir that she called home.

Edom refused to let Israel cross her territory as she travelled to the Promised Land (Numbers 20:14-18). Continuing strife ensued, but David eventually brought her under control (2 Samuel 8:14). Edom later rebelled (2 Kings 8:22) and eventually helped Nebuchadnezzar in his conquest of Judah and Jerusalem. This revenge on Judah cost Edom her complete existence. Vengeance against God's people, even though God Himself was punishing them, brought God's own vengeance upon that neighbouring nation. Philistia was guilty of the same crime: she took vengeance on Judah. God therefore wrought vengeance in return. The Philistines were destined to disappear as a nation altogether. They had originally migrated from Crete; they are referred to as the Kerethites (the Hebrew word is 'keritim'). Ezekiel reported with a play on words that God would cut off (the Hebrew word is 'hikrati') the keritim.

The eastern and western neighbours being accounted for, Ezekiel turns his prophetic utterances against the north, and it is in these four prophecies against Tyre that we see something much deeper. Each one begins with, "The word of the LORD came to me" (Ezekiel 26:1; 27:1; 28:1,11). Not only would God's enemies be abolished, but the one who motivated them against God and the godly would himself eventually be judged. As surely as the neighbours were overturned, so surely will Judah's great enemy know justice. Tyre had been a mighty sea-going nation and a strong commercial rival of Jerusalem, depending on trade by land routes. Tyre rejoiced over Jerusalem's fall, but her shouting was short-lived. God would bring sufficient force against her to sweep her into the sea. After Nebuchadnezzar's onslaught, Alexander the Great reduced her to rubble and even threw that into the Mediterranean. She would be left barren as a place for fishermen to dry their nets. Though Tyre's neighbouring trading partners would greatly mourn, she would never again be found as a nation.

The second prophecy was a poetic lament in which Tyre was compared to a great ship, built with the finest of materials and manned by a stalwart crew. She was described as the perfection of beauty (Ezekiel 27:3) and traded in the finest of the world's goods, but she was headed for shipwreck: 'And you will be no more' (Ezekiel 27:36). Chapter 28 deals with a reigning king, Itobaal II, whose pride, like that of the one who moved him, made him boast as a god. He was even said to be wiser than Daniel (Ezekiel 28:3), but in spite of his boasting he was a mere man; he would die at the hand of strangers. The mouth of the LORD had spoken it (Ezekiel 28:10). It is here that the prophecy takes a deeper meaning. Verses 11-19 take up a lament over one who is called the king of Tyre, describing him in superhuman language, no doubt referring to Satan and his eventual demise, though he is not here mentioned by name.

Described as one who had "the seal of perfection, full of wisdom and perfect in beauty. You were in Eden, the garden of God ..." his privileges and responsibilities were certainly unique; he was created with enormous abilities and treasures, but he was a creature, not a creator. This creature was the anointed cherub that covers and was appointed to the holy mountain of God, blameless. But he sinned and was cast out. The eventual judgement, yet future, reads, "And you will be no more!" This portion deserves special reading. If ever we were tempted to arise in pride, somehow consumed with self-importance and beauty and so knowingly sin against the Almighty Creator, these verses should make us fall before God in grateful appreciation and worship. Satan who sinned found no forgiveness; God in His grace forgives even such as you and me again and again! Satan will be consumed in fire (Revelation 20:10) and will be in a figure as ashes on the earth (Ezekiel 28:18). God will give us and Israel a garland instead of ashes, and the oil of gladness instead of mourning (Isaiah 61:3).

Also on the northern border of Israel, about 20 miles north of Tyre, was Sidon. Sidon, too, must suffer for sins similar to those of her sister city. God would be glorified in her demise, just as He would in Israel's eventual restoration. We remember that these prophecies were spoken largely for the captivity of Judah's benefit. Be that as it may, Sidon, along with the other condemned city-states, would come to know through their judgement that God was the LORD. Judah should have learned that also.

Finally, in chapters 29-32, Ezekiel turns to the south and takes up the word of the LORD against Pharaoh and against Egypt and all her allies and this he does in a series of seven oracles. All of these, except the second, are in chronological order. Egypt was noted for her multitudinous population and chapters 30 to 32 mention those multitudes no less than fourteen times. The vastness of the hordes and the number and strength of the cities carefully enumerated for judgement were no strength against the pronounced doom. However, Egypt was also to be resuscitated; after forty years she would again be populated, but only ever after to be a minor nation, held in check always by the powerful nations that would arise in the east. God has yet a place for her in Israel's future glory. Just as Assyria had been destroyed because of her pride, so Egypt must likewise go to the pit, her aspirations to greatness made empty and worthless by the mighty power of God. Assyria, though a conqueror of Israel's northern kingdom, though compared to a cedar of Lebanon, well-watered and fruitful, had been brought to nothing through Babylon.

The believer today does well to learn the lesson. As Proverbs 16:18 warns us: Pride goes before destruction.

9

GOD'S RESTORATION OF ISRAEL

Seventy years after the fall of Jerusalem the citizens of Israel would be released from captivity and in major movements under Zerubbabel, and later under Ezra, a small remnant return to their land. They would build walls, gates, temple, a priesthood, a nation. Lethargy and apostasy would dog their ambition to godliness (Malachi 1:6-2:17). However, the nation would continue limping along in some sort of fashion until the Lord Jesus was born, lived, was rejected and crucified, taught the truths of the Kingdom for forty days and ascended back to His Father's side.

Rome had a firm grip on the nation by this time, and by A.D. 70 Titus had destroyed what was left of any meaningful temple worship and buildings, though Christ had previously condemned Israel to a Godless temple (Luke 13:35). But God is not finished with Israel by any means, and in spite of all her apostasy and disinterest, in a future day her Messiah will return to earth to take His rightful place over the nation (Zechariah 14:4). While other prophets such as Haggai encouraged them in building after the exile, Ezekiel joined with Isaiah, Jeremiah and Zechariah in looking still further forward to Israel's millennial glory. Ezekiel does this with very specific visions about temple, the priesthood, and the layout of the land.

First, so that a remnant might fully grasp the grace and goodness of God, he iterates the past Israeli history that resulted in her exilic experience (Ezekiel 36:16-21). Israel must be brought to realize that she alone was responsible for her sins and their punishment. Restoration is then described (Ezekiel 36:24ff) and this leads into the vision of the valley of dry bones, replete with the pouring out of the Spirit of God upon the nation and all the magnificence of divine restoration and cleansing. Bloodshed and idolatry were the reasons given for Israel's impurity (Ezekiel 36:17,18), and the extreme seriousness of Israel's sin was that her presence outside of the land that God had given them, a land flowing with milk and honey, provided pollution to the name of the Lord.

It looked as though God had been unable to protect them against the might of Babylon, and a common opinion amongst the nations, if not among the people of Israel themselves, was that God was weak and incapable. In this way, Israel profaned the name to which and by which they had been called (v.20).

How intensely solemn that even in our present day my personal actions and our collective activities either magnify or detract from the appreciated glory of the Almighty! Our lives are seen not only by our neighbours on earth, but by angelic and demonic powers in the heavens! Israel's restoration was to be completed, not by anything that she would be able to accomplish, but according to divine mercy.

God had compassion for His holy name which Israel had profaned (vv.21-23,32). Just as Ezekiel had seen the glory of the Lord departing from the house and the land (Ezekiel 11:14-21), that same glory would return (chapter 43); Israel would once again be the head and not the tail and

God would be glorified in her. His name would no longer be polluted among the nations (Ezekiel 36:22,23). In that day Israel will be restored from all the nations. He will cleanse her from her past bloodshed and idolatry (Jeremiah 33:6-26). Ezekiel 36:26,27 show that the Lord will remove the old heart of stone and give, instead, a heart of flesh, and a new spirit within them (Joel 2:28,29; Ezekiel 37:14). To them God will give the land promised to Abraham (Ezekiel 37:28; Genesis 12:7). The New Covenant will not remove the Old, but will subsume it.

The law will be written on their hearts (Jeremiah 31:33). The land will produce to such an extent that she will know nothing of famine (Ezekiel 34:29; Isaiah 35:1,2). Not only will Israel recognize the Lord's goodness to her, but all other nations will also (Ezekiel 37:28). The vision of the valley of dry bones is not a separate vision, but all part of the same. The words, "And the word of the LORD came to me", are not given here to introduce another thought as they so often are in Ezekiel. The order of God's dealing with them is the same as the order given in Ezekiel 36:22-27: position, then cleansing. Israel, united as seen in the vision of the united sticks, will remain in the land of Israel forever (Genesis17:8).

Never again will Israel defile itself with idols (Ezekiel 37:23); David, or David's greater Son rather, will be their king (Ezekiel 37:24); God's covenant of peace is guaranteed to them, and his sanctuary will be in their midst forever; God will be their God and they will be His people (Ezekiel 37:27). Not only Israel, but all the nations will know that the Lord is the One who sanctifies Israel when His sanctuary is in their midst forever (Ezekiel 37:28).

The interjection at this point of the invasion by, and victory over, Gog in chapters 38 and 39 of Ezekiel presents one of the great difficulties of the book that was mentioned earlier. However, it should not detract from the lessons we can be sure of and can clearly apply. This matter will not be solved by this book, if, in fact, the matter can be resolved before its eventual fulfilment. However, we can expose some of the difficulties that appear and suggest a possible answer. Whatever the result, God's people will be seriously attacked, perhaps more than once, for double fulfilment of Biblical prophecies is not at all unusual. The attack(s) will be repulsed by the Lord in ways obviously supernatural. All the world will know that God is judging; Israel will understand that the Lord is Israel's God (Ezekiel 39:21,22).

The difficulties centre on the time of the attack and the times involved in burying the dead and burning the army's equipment, the trying to align the details with what is recorded in Revelation 20:7ff, and the meaning of such expressions as Israel dwelling in security (Ezekiel 38:8). There seems little point taking months and years to bury and burn if there is to be an immediate resurrection of all the dead for the Great White Throne judgement which is immediately to ensue, followed by the burning up of 2 Peter 3. Ezekiel 39:7,22 declare that the Lord's name will not again be polluted after Gog is defeated.

This rules out pre-Tribulation timing or yet an attack that belongs to the middle or end of Daniel's 70th week, for there will be pollution then even in the temple of God (2 Thessalonians 2:4). Some have postulated a transition period between the Tribulation and the beginning of the Millennium, a time that would allow for the years of burying the dead and burning the armaments (Ezekiel 39:9,12) and this seems logical. However, this argument precludes the Revelation account and the Ezekiel account being one and the same. Revelation 20 definitely occurs at the end of the millennium when Satan has been released from his thousand-year imprisonment. He then will call for the enemies of God to rise up from the ends of the earth and fight against Israel. If the names of Gog and Magog are simply symbolic for the enemies of God there seems little to suggest Ezekiel and John were prophesying concerning the same time period. Predatory animals and birds feasting on the slain (Ezekiel 39:17; Revelation 19:17): might well happen more than once. In any case, there seems no reason to confuse Armaggedon's battle with anything to do with Gog and Magog.

Whatever the answer to these problems, and the Bible doesn't guarantee to answer problems that we imagine, God will defeat all enemies to Himself and His people. As long as Satan is free he will foment the type of trouble described in both cases. When Satan is eventually assigned to the Lake of Fire, eternal peace for God's own, will be fully realized. The present-day people of God are not involved in any of this turmoil, except possibly as onlookers at the judgement of Satan. We shall have long been glorified with the Lord Jesus.

What follows in Ezekiel 40 to 48 is the revelation of actual physical changes that are to be brought about in Israel during millennial days. Some competent commentators have assigned the last eight chapters of the book to the eternal state and have tried to relate similarities accordingly. Though there are similarities, for instance, each describe a river, the descriptions differ. The two cities are different sizes, the sea is a boundary in Ezekiel; while Revelation declares that there is no more sea, and so on. Rightly dividing the word of truth is as necessary in examining prophecy as it is discerning God's will in our present day. The Millennium is in a sense the preparation for the eternal state for Israel. It is not surprising, therefore, if there should be similarities between the two.

10

A WORD TO SHEPHERDS

A very large part of Israel's transgression against God was resident in her leaders, her teachers, her priests, her shepherds, so it is not unreasonable that these be mentioned in detail throughout the book, with inherent lessons for those who have been called to the lead in our own day as well.

God speaks directly through His prophet to the leaders of Israel. He also gives us incidental instruction while dealing with other matters. A succinct lesson is given, for instance, in the lamentation over Tyre. This sea-going nation was compared to a great ship, beautiful and seaworthy, but headed for shipwreck. It was a comparison that seafarers would understand. In her prime, her wise men were her pilots (Ezekiel 27:8); the elders of Gebal and her wise men repaired her seams (verse 9). Those who pilot any great ship must be men of wisdom, which if any man lack, James tells us, (James 1:5) let him ask of God. Dare any pilot of God's people not be continuously asking for the wisdom that is from above? Solomon's request for it at his ascension to the throne greatly pleased the LORD and brought the king and his people great rewards!

Secondly, the elders and wise men together repaired the ship's seams. How necessary in dealing with any people, particularly God's people, is this job of mending seams. We are so apt to fracture apart and Satan would strive to break the unity that is so pleasant to God (Psalm 133). Someone must take the lowly place, a servant of Christ and of others, to go into the undesirable depths of the vessel, right down into the hull, the bilge, to bind and undergird and secure what will otherwise just fly apart under stress of wind and storm and flood. That kind of leadership in Tyre's ship and in ours will draw others to share in that in which we rejoice (verse 9b; Song of Songs 1:4)!

False prophets misled the people by whitewashing walls that should have been cemented with mortar in that they prophesied peace when there was no peace (Ezekiel 13:10-12). Leaders can whitewash walls that should be reconstructed also. Think of Leviticus 14:34ff where infected stones needed to be excised from the dwelling place. Whitewashing would have resulted in the whole building being lost. Correct leadership would have examined and scraped and, if necessary, removed the offending stone. There are obvious temptations to whitewash in God's building today. No favours are given to anyone by not carrying out the necessary!

But direct words to leaders in chapter 20 and onward also would teach men who would lead. Elders on one occasion appeared before Ezekiel to inquire of the Lord (v.1) but He would not be inquired of by them (v.3). Why? God's complaint about them and their fathers was a lack of holiness: "they did not cast away the detestable things of their eyes, nor did they forsake the idols of Egypt" (verse 8). Ezekiel then reviews the different periods in the history of Israel. He rescued them again and again in spite of their rebellion right from Egypt onwards and the current generation was no better. As in the case of many of their kings, they loved righteousness, but they did not hate iniquity. God's Perfect Servant did both (Psalm 45:7; Hebrews 1:9). Restoration and blessing would accompany such leaders only when separation and holiness caused a loathing of defiling deeds as well as the loving of the blessing that attends righteous ones (v.44).

Chapter 19 brings us to a dirge against Israel's more or less current leaders through two figures, a lion and her whelps and a vine and its branches. The lion is a figure of Judah; the first of her whelps, Jehoahaz, is cited for his wickedness, the devouring of mankind. His punishment is to be taken captive in chains to Egypt by Pharaoh Neco and to die there. The next whelp is Jehoiakin. (Jehoiakim, who followed Jehoahaz, is missed out here, perhaps not quite as evil as the others.) Jehoiakin's evil is also the devouring of men and cities. Ezekiel prophesied a lion hunt, which would bring the necessary judgement.

The second figure is that of Judah as a vine. No specific ruler is designated by the rods that grew out of the vine, but a picture of fruitfulness withering to dried up, transplanted wastefulness gives a picture of Judah being carried off to the desert, Babylon, because of her wicked leaders. How solemn, once again, to realize that leadership affects not only the life of the leader, but the lives of followers, either for fruitfulness or for blasted fruitlessness. The effects of poor leadership are not only temporal, but eternal!

As a result of untrue leadership, judgement was now to fall upon all the land. A thorough history of unjust leadership was now given to those in captivity (Ezekiel 20:5-44) and with it an assurance that Judah would get no benefit from relying upon Egypt for help. That is where the whole problem had started in the first place. Ezekiel's message was one of the necessity of repentance. Jerusalem's leaders had their failures listed in every category (Ezekiel 22:1-31): They had broken the demands of the covenant; they had misused their positions to lord it over the flock and this resulted in people being put to death unjustly; they had treated their parents without due honour; they had oppressed strangers. They had maltreated widows and orphans, despised the Sabbath, used slander, worshipped idols, behaved immorally, taken bribes and overtaxed the common people and charged undue interest.

This was all summed up in the Lord's words in verse 12: "But you have forgotten Me." There is little point keeping the feasts of the Lord and disregarding the commandments of the Lord. No point saying, "Lord, Lord," and not doing the things that He says (Luke 6:46)! There is little point keeping the remembrance of the Lord today and nullifying the requisite holiness, either personal or ecclesiastical! Leaders, shepherds take note! We teach those in the church by example as well as by precept!

One of the great problems in Israel and Judah was the existence of false prophets, men who spoke as though from God, but lacking in communion with Him. They resembled lions that devoured the innocent, denying refreshment and encouragement from the Lord to people anxiously awaiting it, announcing that the people should go to war when God had not commanded it. The nation therefore hungered when it might have been fed. Men were needlessly slain, multiplying the number of fatherless and widows in the land. Those who followed in leadership had learned from their forebears, with the few exceptions being specially mentioned as those who did well, but far outnumbered by ravenous wolves that did not spare the flock. God spare us from empty teachers and ravenous leaders among us today! In Israel's day God looked in vain for a leader who would stand against all and for Him. They would all be held to account in judgement!

The chapter on shepherds (34) speaks of those who fleece the sheep instead of feeding them. "Should not the shepherds feed the flock?" (Ezekiel 34:2). Secondly, when sheep wandered astray the shepherds did not "search or seek for them" (Ezekiel 34:7). God places Himself against such shepherds. The recipe for a good shepherd is seen in God's description of what He Himself will do: search, care for them on a gloomy day, lead them to a place of rest. It is in this context that this great promise is written: "And I will make them and the places around My hill a blessing. And I will cause showers to come down in their season; they will be showers of blessing" (Ezekiel 34:26). We pray for showers of blessing. Good shepherding may well lead to them. Then will the flock rejoice in the experience of David: "The LORD is my shepherd, I shall not want" (Psalm 23:1).

In chapter 40 in the middle of revealing truths concerning the new millennial temple God gives the prescription for a good leader: "Moreover ... teach My people the difference between the holy and the profane and cause them to discern between the clean and the unclean. And in a dispute they shall take their stand to judge; they shall judge it according to My ordinances. They shall also keep My laws and My statutes ..." (Ezekiel 44:23,24). This will make a worthy servant, a worthy leader, a worthy minister of the Word of God.

11

THE LORD IS THERE

It is not without significance that Ezekiel's introduction to Millennial restoration is the building of a new house for God. The first temple had been built by Solomon on Mount Moriah on ground purchased by David from Araunah the Jebusite and according to instructions from God given in writing to David's son. This temple was defiled by Israel and subsequently destroyed by Nebuchadnezzar at the fall of Jerusalem.

A second somewhat inferior-looking structure was erected in the days after the return from exile, encouraged by Haggai and Zechariah and erected under Zerubbabel and Joshua. The temple that was in existence when the Lord was on the earth was built by Herod with Jewish permission. It was destroyed by the Romans under Titus in A.D.70 according to the prophecy of Daniel (Daniel 9:26). While its stones were not left one upon another, as prophesied by Christ (Matthew 24:2), the foundation built by Solomon still exists. Before Antichrist can set up his abomination of desolation (Matthew 24:15; 2 Thessalonians 2:4; Revelation 11:1) another temple, a fourth, will be set up on this site. None of these has been or will be built according to the dimensions and blueprints of Ezekiel's prophecy.

They await a fifth temple, in which, says Isaiah 66:23: "And it shall be from new moon to new moon and from sabbath to sabbath, all mankind will come to bow down before Me,' says the LORD." It would seem that this temple will not be built on the former site, but on top of the mountains in the middle of the priests' part of the holy oblation, a 25,000 reed (about 5 miles) square area (Ezekiel 40:1-5). The sanctuary will be somewhat north of the city. The area where Solomon's temple had been built had been defiled with the graves of the kings of Judah (Ezekiel 43:7,8). (Details apart, we repeat that it is not without significance that the house is mentioned first, for worship in the house has always been foremost in the mind of God! Those who returned from the exile had learned this also (Ezra 3:7ff)).

How blessed to be part of it in a spiritual sense today! But even this temple of Ezekiel with its sacrifices will eventually be done away. 2 Peter 3:7 tells us that both heavens and earth will disappear in a burning maelstrom. With Peter, we look for a new heavens and a new earth wherein righteousness dwells. Peter's admonition (2 Peter 3:11) is of significance here as we consider such things! In that new creation, the eternal state, there will be no physical temple, but the tabernacle of God will be among men; He will dwell among His people (Revelation 21:3). Ezekiel 40-48 show that temporary state, the Millennium, that 'preparation' for Israel for that which will surely follow.

The construction is very detailed, without the gold and sparkle of previous dwelling places. That won't be needed to show God's glory, for the Christ of God will be there. It is only when the house is ready that the glory of God is again seen approaching and entering the house (Ezekiel 43:1-7). The present eastern gate of the city is not the one that the glory of the Lord will enter (Ezekiel 43:4). New structures and new topography will have replaced present situations before that time. There seems no doubt whatever that actual animal sacrifices will once again be offered for Israel (Ezekiel 43:18-27). The best suggestion as to why this should be reinstated (with some variation from Leviticus) during the thousand years is that they might be a memorial only to bring Israel again to a full knowledge of the Lord, and somehow an appreciation of the fulfillment of these types in the sacrifice of Christ at Calvary.

In the new service of worship outlined in chapter 44, some have considered the prince to be Messiah Himself, but this is impossible. He is described in Ezekiel 45:22 as having to offer a sin offering for himself and the people. Messiah has never had to, and shall never have to offer sin offering on His own behalf! Also Ezekiel 46:16 speaks of his having sons. He is perhaps a special representative of Messiah in the kingdom, possibly David himself. Those of the tribe of Levi who had served idols in their lifetime will not be given the right to serve in the Millennial priesthood in the temple, but will appear as overseers in the gate according to the mercy of God.

Again we meet the truth that what we do down here in life will have an effect on the nearness that we enjoy to God and Christ after this life is over. A solemn warning to present-day servants of the Lord! The sons of Zadok who were faithful in times of apostasy will comprise the officiating priesthood. One of the solemn duties of the priesthood then will be to teach the people the difference between the holy and profane, the clean and the unclean. The responsibility to do the same applies today as well! God's millennial house will be protected by a surrounding area about eight miles square and an area for the priests that extends another eight miles east and west. Two walls also separate the house from that which is outside, even in the Millennium.

There is a lesson here about the separation of the house! Again the law of the house (Ezekiel 43:12) in that day should give us reflection on the sanctity of His house today! Special mention of ample support for those who serve should also motivate the generosity of God's people today towards those who so willingly dispense their energies in the service of God's house. The very complete detail concerning the house, its furniture, its feasts and its priesthood, displays the fact that the concern of God that was given to minute detail in the tabernacle and Solomon's temple hasn't changed; the detail of the house today is likewise very important. We disregard it at our peril.

Topographical changes in the land of Israel also take place as millennial glory floods the scene. Among other things, a river proceeds from the threshold of the house of God and flows eastward (Ezekiel 47:1). (Zechariah further reports that it will flow westward to the Mediterranean also (Zechariah 14:8)). Beginning as a trickle (v.2), it gains strength and depth, and within a few thousand cubits (about 2 miles) it becomes waters in which one could swim. Detail is not given in vain in Scripture: as we walk through the purifying blessing that ever flows from God's presence we will find our ankles and walk affected, our knees and prayer life affected, our loins and spiritual propagation affected, and soon we will experience such blessings that we are able to completely submerge ourselves in them.

These waters of Ezekiel 47 will bring life to the Dead Sea and fruitfulness to arid plains of the Arabah, bringing health and healing to the nations, and fish in abundance wherever the river flows (vv.7-9). It's interesting that the river flows in the land of what had been Judah rather than northward to the rest of Israel. There is a similarity purposed in the blessing that flows from the house of God today (Ephesians 4:12), however poorly we enter into God's purpose through us. These prophecies were given as encouragement to the exiled captives of Babylonia.

Land allotments for the various tribes will run from west to east across the land with Dan in the north, followed by Asher, Naphtali, Manasseh, Ephraim and Reuben. Then the territory for the sanctuary, priests, city and prince, is followed by Judah, Benjamin, Simeon, Issachar, Zebulun and Gad. The arrangement is different from what is recorded in Joshua chapters 13-17, or yet from their position in the march towards the Promised Land. While no reason is given for this, we remark again that what happens down here now will affect what takes place hereafter. Then, at last, the territory promised to Abraham will be fully occupied. The land of Israel will be much larger than it ever has been, and will be topographically different also (Zechariah 14). The city that stands in the midst will have 12 gates, three on each side. The tribe of Levi will be represented here, Joseph's gate taking the place of those named for Ephraim and Manasseh (Ezekiel 48:31,32).

This city is not to be confused with the New Jerusalem which shall descend as a bride adorned for her husband in the eternal state (Revelation 21:2), nor is the river of Ezekiel 47 to be confused with the river of Revelation 22, however similar they may seem to be. The name of the Millennial city will be "Yahweh shammah" - "The LORD is there". The presence of the LORD will bring the promised majestic glory to Israel. How sad that they had to spend millennia without it!

12

AN AMAZING TRANSFORMATION (KARL SMITH)

"They will say, 'This land that was desolate has become like the Garden of Eden; and the wasted, desolate, and ruined cities are now ... inhabited'" (Ezekiel 36:35 NKJV).

This verse makes me think of the Great Fire of London in 1666, which destroyed a huge area of the English capital, including many of its most important buildings. Nevertheless, the utter devastation forced a re-building of the city in which destitute areas were replaced with glorious architecture such as Christopher Wren's city churches and St. Paul's Cathedral.

When Ezekiel wrote these words, it must have seemed even more as if it was all over for Jerusalem. The people had persisted in worshipping idols instead of the one true God who cared about them. They were exhausting the land by refusing to obey God's command to let it rest every seventh year and eventually God decided that enough was enough. If they would not give the land these sabbath years, He would take it from them and allow it to rest (2 Chronicles 36:14-21). The Babylonians marched in and took all but the feeblest Jews captive to the capital of their empire, thousands of miles away. The once majestic city of Jerusalem was besieged and systematically destroyed: "the Chaldeans burned the king's house, and the houses of the people with fire, and broke down the walls of Jerusalem" (Jeremiah 39:8).

A waste land and a ruined city. It should all have been so different; it had all been so different, but they had messed it up and it was apparently gone forever. Into this hopeless situation came the word of the LORD. It must have defied belief that the heap of smouldering ruins was going to become a great and protected city once again, where people would live in happiness and safety. Yet Ezekiel believed it. It must have seemed incredible that the barren place should become rich and beautiful and spill over with life and contentment. But this is exactly what God makes it His business to do. Within seventy years, a Jewish remnant went back to rebuild the city and the holy temple where men and women would once again worship God. An amazing transformation was on the way.

And God has not stopped making amazing transformations. Before we were saved, we were dead before God and our lives gave no pleasure to Him or lasting satisfaction to us. Then, the Lord Jesus came and gave us life to the full (John 10:10). Ezekiel was promised a garden and a city. The deserted place would not only grow crops, but be like the Garden of Eden, stocked to bursting with the choicest fruits imaginable. Mankind lost out on the Paradise of Eden when Adam disobeyed God and the human condition has been desolate since. The same disobedience and isolation from the blessings God longed to give to us has been enacted in every human life. Shut out of God's presence, only a lost eternity awaited us.

When the Lord Jesus took the punishment for that disobedience, He made the way back from the desolate to the fruitful. We, too, have been promised a garden and a vibrant city. The Bible tells us of the New Jerusalem which God will bring from heaven at the beginning of a new eternal age: "In the middle of its street, and on either side of the river, was the tree of life, which bore twelve fruits, each tree yielding its fruit every month. The leaves of the tree were for the healing of the nations" (Revelation 22:2 NKJV).

This tree was in the Garden of Eden (Genesis 2:9) and will be there then. The Lord has given us back what we lost through our sin. In fact, He has given us something better. The city will be an amazing place, made of pure, translucent gold (Revelation 21:18), lit up with the glory of the Lamb (v.23) and the famous pearly gates (v.21). Best of all, the Lord Jesus Himself will live there "and His servants shall serve Him. They shall see His face" (Revelation 22:3-4 NKJV).

The God who says, "Behold, I make all things new" (Revelation 21:5 NKJV) is still restoring desolate and ruined lives. Sometimes as Christians, we let what should be productive lives that bring pleasure to God become sterile, empty and ruined. Perhaps like the exiled Israelites, we feel that we've displeased God too badly, too shamefully, too often. Perhaps we even look at our condition, both as individuals and as a community of churches in which God has promised to live amongst his people, and imagine it's too far gone - that He can do nothing with it.

Nevertheless, He is always regenerating, always restoring those who acknowledge their brokenness and complete dependence upon Him. Let's make sure we're daily admitting our helplessness before God and letting Him build something, grow something in our lives that pleases Him: "the nations ... around you shall know that I, the LORD, have rebuilt the ruined places and planted what was desolate. I ... have spoken it, and I will do it" (Ezekiel 36:36 NKJV).

13

WATERS TO SWIM IN (GUY JARVIE)

In Ezekiel 47 we read that the prophet saw in a vision waters issuing out from under the threshold of the house of God. Wonderful waters they were, for, wherever they flowed they brought life (verse 9). On each side of the river grew every kind of fruit tree, bearing fruit each month, and the leaves of the trees never withered. Fish lived abundantly wherever the waters flowed, and the fruit trees bore abundant fruit to eat, and the leaves for healing. Wonderful waters indeed! (verse 12).

Another remarkable thing about this stream was its increasing volume and depth. At a thousand cubits it was ankle deep, and a thousand cubits further on, it had risen to the knees. A thousand cubits further, and it had risen to the waist. A thousand cubits more, and it was a river beyond a man's depth, waters to swim in. Today the river is of another kind, but its effect is similar, after a spiritual sort. The Lord Jesus spoke thus "He that believeth on Me, as the Scripture hath said, out of his belly shall flow rivers of living water. But this spake He of the Spirit" (John 7:38,39). It is the word of God flowing out from us in the power of the Spirit of God, from you, and from me. In Ezekiel we read that the waters came out from under the threshold of the house of God. God intends that out from His people His word should flow in the power of the Spirit. Much has been committed to us, and much is expected from us.

The amazing thing about the waters that Ezekiel saw was their life-sustaining qualities. There was life wherever they flowed. That is the amazing thing too about the word of God in the power of the Spirit of God. Men live when they hear it. Saints are refreshed when they hear it. Lives are changed when the word of God is spoken in the power of the Spirit of God. Spiritual sicknesses are healed, and the saints dwell joyfully together in unity. There is food and healing in such words.

What brings this life-giving power to our words? How can we know the power of the Holy Spirit in our lives and witness? It is close contact with Christ that brings it. In Ezekiel, the waters flowed along the south of the altar (verse 1). The Lord Jesus said, "He that believeth on Me ... out of his belly shall flow rivers of living water." Christ-centred ministry is always powerful. Ministry may be scriptural, and well thought out, and yet powerless, lacking in the life-sustaining quality. No healing in its "leaves", and no food in its "fruit." It will be so, if in some respect it lacks relation to Christ.

Another notable thing about the river that Ezekiel saw was its depth: it had waters to swim in. True, there was the shallow part, but this led on to the depths. We too must have the "shallows," for there are young ones among us who need the first principles of the oracles of Christ. God has provided the shallows for the young and immature. They are right in their time and place, but the depths are for the perfect, for the full-grown. Then also the waters in the shallows had the same life-sustaining qualities as those in the depths. The refreshing words from young men who are in touch with Christ are life-giving. How delightful it is to hear a young and immature brother telling what he knows of Christ! It is all so fresh, and life-sustaining too, and we all enjoy such words.

> "'Tis oft the very simplest word
> That leads a sinner to the Lord.
> God makes simplicity prevail
> When arguments most powerful fail."

But we do not want all shallows. We want the river that flows out from us to deepen as we go forward. Young men who walk with God will deepen in their appreciation of Him, and their ministry will become "waters to the knees." As they deepen in faith and prayer, just so much will they deepen in power in their service. We long to hear and read more of the ministry that corresponds to the "waters to swim in," the kind of ministry that awes our spirits, and makes us bow in adoration of God "Whose every act pure blessing is, His path unsullied light."

Ministry in depth and power causes us to fall in adoration before God, as those heavenly beings do of whom we read in Revelation 4 and 5. How shall we reach such depths in our lives and ministry? By dwelling deep in prayer and faith, not merely by a mental knowledge of the word! If we are shallow in prayer, then we shall be shallow in our ministry, for the two are linked together. "We will continue stedfastly in prayer, and in the ministry of the word," said the apostles Acts (6:4). If we are shallow in faith, then we shall lack power. It was through faith, not through knowledge merely, that some subdued kingdoms (Hebrews 11:33).

Let us dwell deep. Let the roots of our spiritual nature go well down through faith and prayer. This present age would leave us little time for prayer; and an all-embracing insurance system would leave us little need for faith. But prayer and faith are the two great essentials for depth in our spiritual beings. Without these we are bound to be shallow and powerless. We need waters to swim in. We need the abundant life of which the Lord has spoken (John 10:10). We need the rivers of living water to flow out through us to others. If we are satisfied with nothing but these, then God will grant them to us.

14

A THANKLESS TASK (BOB ARMSTRONG)

"A rebellious nation ... impudent children and stiffhearted ... and they, whether they will hear, or whether they will forbear ... yet shall know that there hath been a prophet among them. And thou, son of man, be not afraid of them" (Ezekiel 2:3-6, KJV).

The thunder of Babylonian armed forces had been heard at the gates of Jerusalem; Nebuchadnezzar shook the earth as he conquered. Judah and Benjamin, favoured tribes of Israel, fell to his conquest. Although this despot ruler of a world empire was God's instrument of judgement, it was disobedience to the word of the Lord and idolatry that brought Judah to Babylon.

As the captives sat reflecting by the rivers of Babylon, perhaps of their past glory, there was amongst them a man of priestly bearing (Ezekiel 1:3), who saw visions of incredible brightness and glory. He was prostrated before the Lord, and out of the vision came the voice of God to his heart. He was sent to a people who were already paying in exile years the price exacted for choosing their own way instead of God's. No doubt as the prophet sat among the captives he heard their conversation, and it may have gone something like this. Why should we listen to a prophet now? At least there is safety in Babylon. They were free from the sound and terror of invading armies, free from the spectre of want and famine. No longer did they hear the cry of hungry children, whom it was easier to kill than feed. No longer were ruthless assaults made on the privacy of domestic life (2 Chronicles 36).

The broad rivers of Babylon were pleasant, and as the months slipped past, life became easier and more settled. It was only the godly few amongst them who longed for the courts of the Lord's house, which no doubt to many had become but a memory. Into this environment Ezekiel the prophet is commissioned to project his flaming message of judgement to his exiled people. The success of his ministry was not to be measured in terms of those who flocked to his side in repentance, for there appeared none. Measured by the standards of modern evangelism, his ministry would be considered a failure. However, it was rather that God had spoken and His prophet had been sent amongst them. What really mattered for the moment was that his message had been faithfully delivered, whether they heard or not. Rest assured, God's word will not return void! Far out across the centuries of time these eternal words will ring out. Neither the hosts of hell, nor the currents of history will ever hush them. They will stand up in the judgements of Israel and the world to condemn all who ignore them or trifle with them: "If thou warn the wicked, and he turn not from his wickedness, nor from his wicked way, he shall die in his iniquity; but thou hast delivered thy soul" (Ezekiel 3:19 RV).

Reading the record we are impressed with the formidable task Ezekiel had towards an obstinate people, who refused to listen. We need men like Ezekiel for our own times; men who have heard the voice of God and are not afraid to speak His truth. Men who are on God's side because they know God is on their side. As the darkness deepens around us, pray that He will give us men who will spend their lives under the shadow of the Almighty, and throw themselves on the resources of the Holy Spirit, and come out with anointed lips to speak His message, to break the bondage of whatever is preventing us from knowing the fulness of the Spirit in our lives and ministry.

There is a different yet similar crisis in this twentieth century, when floods of ungodliness and immorality would seep into the sanctity of our personal lives. While looking back and preaching about the failures of God's people in earlier times, we may well be unaware of the spiritual paralysis of our own times. The subtle intrusion of more and more legitimate and harmless things into our lives is greatly reducing our spiritual perception and power. A renewal of practical holiness and detachment from the World in the possessive sense, will result only as the interior life glows with the fire of love and obedience to the Lord.

Such is God's answer to stem the tides which threaten to bring sin and compromise amongst the people of God in these latter days. Are we willing to pay the price of cleansing "from all defilement of flesh and spirit, perfecting holiness in the fear of God" (2 Corinthians 7:1 RV)? "Love not the world (Greek: 'kosmos', world system), neither the things that are in the world" (1 John 2:15 RV). This includes the religious as well as the secular system and its pleasures. These are some of the prerequisites of a revival ministry from the Lord.

> "Revive Thy work, O Lord,
> Thy mighty arm make bare.
> Speak with the voice that wakes the dead;
> First make Thy people hear.
> Revive Thy work, O Lord,

Disturb this sleep of death.
Quicken the smouldering embers,
Lord, By Thine almighty breath.
Revive Thy work, O Lord,
Create soul thirst for Thee.
And hungering for the bread of life,
Oh, may our spirits be!"

15

EZEKIEL'S WIFE (IAN LITHGOW)

We read about her in the book that bears his name (Ezekiel 24:18). This is the only place in the whole prophecy where she is directly mentioned. The house Ezekiel speaks of in 3:24 and 8:1 was the one they shared together. As far as we know, they did not have any children. She meant much to the prophet of God, who was also a priest (Ezekiel 1:3). As a prophet he served God from the age of perhaps 30 (Ezekiel 1:1) to at least his 52nd year (see Ezekiel 1:2 regarding the commencing date; Ezekiel 29:17 shows the last recorded date of his prophetic office).

God describes Ezekiel's wife as "the desire of thine eyes". The word desire is translated as lovely (Song of Songs 5:16), "Yea, He is altogether lovely", describing both the moral and physical beauty found in a person. She was the ideal helpmeet and we can picture the home they shared and their deep love for God's things.

God was going to test his servant's faith by taking away what was very precious and dear to him, namely, his wife. He was not elderly when this occurred (see Ezekiel 24:1, where the year is the ninth year of captivity). It is suggested that, in Ezekiel 1:1, the thirtieth year is that of the prophet's age. The prophet states in Ezekiel 1:2 that he had been in captivity 5 years. By a comparison of these scriptures we conclude that Ezekiel was thirty-four when the word of the Lord came to him: "Son of man, behold, I take away from thee the desire of thine eyes with a stroke: yet neither shalt thou mourn nor weep, neither shall thy tears run down" (RV). Many times the word of God had come to him and the Lord's message was faithfully proclaimed, whether of blessing, instruction, or judgement. Never had such a personal word as this been communicated to him. This would touch the innermost parts of his being. Where some may question the working of God, this noble servant said, "So I spake unto the people in the morning; and at even my wife died: and I did in the morning as I was commanded". Here was a test of faith. Ezekiel passed through with full marks and stands beside the other great men and women of faith.

Behind it all was the purpose of God in speaking to His people concerning the desire of their eyes. A far different context this was from the Lord's description of the prophet's desire. The Lord's message is delivered by Ezekiel in 24:21 (RV) following their enquiry concerning the death of his wife and its meaning to them. The word to them was, "Thus saith the Lord GOD: Behold, I will profane My sanctuary, the pride of your power, the desire of your eyes, and that which your soul pitieth". Although they were captives in Babylon, their affection and trust were centred on the city of Jerusalem, believing that they would soon return. Instead of turning to God for forgiveness and strength they trusted in the fortifications of Jerusalem. Now they were going to hear of the destruction that would come upon the city. Ezekiel was a sign to them. As his wife was taken away and he did not mourn for her, so they would be silent when the news came concerning the city. Then they would know that the Lord God alone was their ruler and He alone should be their trust.

God spoke through a faithful man. The cost was great and we are not told of the prophet's sadness, but God knew. He would not allow His servant to pass through what He Himself was not willing to accept. The day came when the One who was all the Father's delight - our Lord Jesus Christ - went to Golgotha's cross and there had all our iniquity laid upon Him.

If in our experience we are called to pass through the waters of tribulation or the fire of testing, what will be our reaction? Will it be a complaining spirit, turning back, or the quiet confidence of the Psalmist, "Yea, though I walk through the valley of the shadow of death, I will fear no evil; for Thou art with me". May what was true of faithful Ezekiel characterize us. "At even my wife died: and I did in the morning as I was commanded".

16

THE HANDS OF A MAN (GUY JARVIE)

"They had the hands of a man under their wings" (Ezekiel 1:8). The book of Ezekiel is a rich mine to those who take time to dig in it. Much of its prophecy may be hidden from us now, because it belongs to Israel, and to a future day. Yet some of it we can enjoy. We feel, as we read it, how very finite we are.

We read of those heavenly beings who went whithersoever the Spirit was to go. Each one of them had four faces and four wings. They were like the seraphim, of whom we read in Isaiah 6:6, their appearance was as burning coals of fire (1:18). They ran and returned as the appearance of a flash of lightning. There is much about them that we cannot understand, and much that is awesome. The noise of their wings was like the noise of great waters. But under their wings they had the hands of a man.

Above the living creatures was the likeness of a throne, and the likeness of the appearance of a Man upon it above. It is not possible for us to understand such descriptions, but we know what like the hands of a man are. The appearance of a Man upon the throne, we judge to be one of the appearances of our Lord Jesus Christ. When Ezekiel saw all this he fell upon his face.

"The hands of a man"! This may speak to us of men being linked with heavenly beings in fulfilling the eternal purposes of God. Brother, sister, your hands are needed to work with the Divine Spirit! Where? In the world! We read of those living creatures that "they went every one straight forward: whither the Spirit was to go, they went" (1:12 RV). Shall we go where the Spirit leads? We cannot go alone, or on our own initiative. We must go where and when the Spirit leads.

Like Isaiah, Ezekiel saw the vision first, and then came the word of the LORD, "Son of man, I send thee." Is the Lord likely to send us, as He sent Ezekiel? Not unless we are quiet before Him as Ezekiel was. He was upon his face when he first heard the Voice.

In chapter 3 he receives the word that he is to speak, "Thus saith the Lord GOD; whether they will hear, or whether they will forbear" (Ezekiel 3:11 RV). This is an important lesson for the servant of Christ today. He is to speak the word of the Lord, and to speak it with authority. He is not to colour it, nor to give any of his own imagination, nor is he to try and make it pleasing to men. It is God's word to be carried faithfully and feelingly to the people. "Son of man," He said, "go, get thee to them."

But how will he go? "Then the Spirit lifted me up, and I heard behind me the voice of a great rushing, saying, Blessed be the glory of the LORD from His place" (3:12 RV). It is the servant of the LORD being carried forward irresistibly to do the work of the LORD, carried where the Spirit would have him to go.

Those who have travelled by plane will have felt the thrill as the plane is taking off, and the maximum power is being exerted by the engines to make it rise. It feels almost like a living thing, as the traveller is borne upward and onward to his destination. So it was as the man Ezekiel was borne upward, as if on the wings of the living creatures, their wings being joined to each other. "So," he said, "the Spirit lifted me up, and took me away" (Ezekiel 3:14 RV).

Surely we will not sit at ease in this the last hour! In Mark 16.20 (RV), we read, "They went forth, and preached everywhere, the Lord working with them." Ezekiel says, "I came to them ... where they dwelt" (Ezekiel 3:15 RV). Where they dwell! Yes, that is where we must go, not by some impulse of our own, but borne there by the Spirit of God. God was at work and He was working through His servant. Mighty heavenly beings were at work, but they had the hands of a man under their wings. God was with this man who was carrying His word to the people (Israel) where they dwelt.

As Ezekiel sat there among the people, the word of the LORD came to him. "Son of man, I have made thee a watchman unto the house of Israel: therefore hear the word at My mouth, and give them warning from Me" (Ezekiel 3:17 RV). The prophet could not possibly evade that word. He was a responsible man to pass on the word of the LORD to the people to whom God had sent him. Let the words of Ezekiel 3 ring in our ears until we see our responsibility, not only to the favoured few in English-speaking lands, but to the multitudes elsewhere, who sit in darkness and the shadow of death. We think of the words of Paul, "I testify unto you this day, that I am pure from the blood of all men" (Acts 20:26 RV). What part are we taking to reach "the millions"? Many dear brethren will say, "We have been preaching this word from our youth". Thank God for that. Do not cease until the Master comes.

Lest Ezekiel should tire of continually warning the people, the word of the LORD came again to him in chapter 33:7 (RV), "Son of man, I have set thee a watchman unto the house of Israel; therefore hear the word at My mouth, and give them warning from Me." Brethren, continue in your faithful ministry at home and abroad, whether the people hear you, or refuse to hear you. Continue in your faithful ministry. Dear younger brethren, you have youth and health and zeal and adaptability. Is the Lord calling you? Can you hear a cry from across the seas, "Come over and help us or we die"? Someone has written:

> "Facing a task unfinished
> That drives us to our knees,
> A need that undiminished
> Rebukes our slothful ease.
> We who rejoice to know Thee,
> Renew before Thy throne,
> The solemn pledge we owe Thee
> To make Thy glory known.
>
> Where other lords beside Thee
> Hold their unhindered sway;
> Where forces that defied Thee,
> Defy Thee still today.
> With none to heed their crying
> For life and love and light,
> Unnumbered souls are dying
> And pass into the night."

MORE TITLES FROM HAYES PRESS

You may be interested to know that Hayes Press has many more books for you to enjoy. For example, our Search For Truth series by Brian Johnston contains excellent reading material in a down-to-earth and conversational style, covering a wide range of topics from Bible character studies, theme studies, book studies, apologetics, prophecy, Christian living and more. Hayes Press also has its own imprint and our ever-increasing catalogue includes the following which you may be interested in:

Precious Facets: The Bible Names and Titles of Jesus (Volumes 1 & 2)

The Apostle Peter once said that "there is no other name under heaven that has been given among men by which we must be saved." Such a name must be well worth finding out about! The name that Peter referred to was Jesus Christ the Nazarene, but He was, and is, known by many different names. In this devotional and meditational book, twelve different authors write about twenty-six of them. Some of Jesus' names were given by God, some by men and some He gave Himself, but each name tells us something valuable and precious about His character, His Person or His work. The Apostle Paul said of a future day that "at the name of Jesus every knee will bow". This book has been published to encourage its readers to do so today - and every day.

Bible Covenants 101

The topic of "Bible Covenants" might seem to be an unusual subject, but it's vitally important to get to grips with to understand how God wants to have a relationship with mankind. This little guide is a perfect way to get a quick introduction to the subject. The first chapter reviewing the main components of the Biblical covenant with the following chapters taking a look at the main covenants in the Bible, as well as some lesser well-known ones. The final chapters analyse the progression of these covenants from Old to New Testament, from the Old Covenant to the New Covenant, and the final chapter concludes the book with a look at the relevance of the use of the word "Testament". Why do we have Old and New Testaments and how is this related to covenants?

Different Discipleship: Jesus' Sermon on the Mount

A practical, challenging study (complete with questions and prayer prompts) of the "Sermon on the Mount" for followers and would-be followers of Jesus. What makes Jesus and his followers "different"? Find out why this revolutionary, life-changing sermon is why Jesus Christ is regarded as one of the world's most important teachers, even by those who don't follow him as their Lord and Saviour.

The Battle: An Anthology of Spiritual Warfare (Volumes 1 & 2)

In this eclectic collection, 24 writers join forces over two volumes to provide training, a call to arms and a mission briefing on this vital topic for every Christian. As a special feature, each chapter is followed by a piece of poetry, a hymn, a pithy thought or some "battle quotes". Equally perfect as an aid to individual devotions or as a study resource!

A Study in Prophetic Principles

Do you find Bible prophecy to be a confusing subject? Would you like to be able to understand Bible prophecy about the end times, not just in the book of Revelation, but in the Bible books of Daniel, Ezekiel and others as well? In this concise Bible commentary, George Prasher provides the keys to Bible prophecy by exploring and explaining the underlying principles and patterns in four main sections:

1. The significance and range of prophecy in the plan of divine revelation
2. Patterns of prophetic presentation
3. The main themes of Bible prophecy
4. A study of false prophecy

This is an ideal book if you are planning to start a prophecy Bible study, either personally or as a group.

ABOUT HAYES PRESS

Hayes Press (www.hayespress.org) is a registered charity in the United Kingdom, whose primary mission is to disseminate the Word of God, mainly through literature. It is one of the largest distributors of gospel tracts and leaflets in the United Kingdom, with over 100 titles and many thousands dispatched annually. In addition to paperbacks and eBooks, Hayes Press also publishes Plus Eagles' Wings, a fun and educational Bible magazine for children, and Golden Bells, a popular daily Bible reading calendar in wall or desk formats.

If you would like to contact Hayes Press, there are a number of ways you can do so:

By mail: c/o The Barn, Flaxlands, Royal Wootton Bassett, Wiltshire, UK SN4 8DY

By phone: 01793 850598

By eMail:info@hayespress.org

via Facebook: www.facebook.com/hayespress.org

www.ingramcontent.com/pod-product-compliance
Lightning Source LLC
Chambersburg PA
CBHW071407040426
42444CB00009B/2141